Riches of the Earth

Tomatoes

Irene Franck and David Brownstone

GROLIER

An imprint of Scholastic Library Publishing
Danbury, Connecticut

Credits and Acknowledgments

abbreviations: t (top), b (bottom), l (left), r (right), c (center)

Image credits: Agricultural Research Service Library: 4, 8, and 28 (Scott Bauer), 16l and 16r (Jack Dykinga), 19 (Keith Weller), 20; Art Resource: 12 (Pierpont Morgan Library, MA3900, f.7v), 15 (Giraudon); Getty Images: 11 (Image Bank/Robert Earnest), 21 (Stone/Wayne Eastep), 24r (Stone/Chris Thomaidis), 26r (Foodpix/Burke/ Triolo Productions); Getty Images/PhotoDisc: 1b, 5, and 6l (detail) (John A. Rizzo), 9 (PhotoLink/Kent Knudson), 18 (Ryan McVay), 26l (Mitch Hrdlicka), 27 (Jess Alford); Library of Congress: 13; John Marshall: 22; National Aeronautics and Space Administration (NASA): 1t and running heads; Photo Researchers, Inc.: 6r (Holt Studios International), 7l (Jerome Wexler), 10r (Alan and Linda Detrick), 29 (Tom Myers); U.S. Department of Agriculture: 7r (Alice Welch), 10l (Bill Tarpenning), 14 (Ken Hammond), 24l and 25 (David F. Warren); World Bank: 3 (Curt Carnemark). Original image drawn for this book by K & P Publishing Services: 23.

Our thanks to Joe Hollander, Phil Friedman, and Laurie McCurley at Scholastic Library Publishing; to photo researchers Susan Hormuth, Robin Sand, and Robert Melcak; to copy editor Michael Burke; and to the librarians throughout the northeastern library network, in particular to the staff of the Chappaqua Library— director Mark Hasskarl; the expert reference staff, including Martha Alcott, Michele J. Capozzella, Maryanne Eaton, Catherine Paulsen, Jane Peyraud, Paula Peyraud, and Carolyn Reznick; and the circulation staff, headed by Barbara Le Sauvage—for fulfilling our wide-ranging research needs.

Published 2003 by Grolier
Division of Scholastic Library Publishing
Old Sherman Turnpike
Danbury, Connecticut 06816

For information address the publisher:
Scholastic Library Publishing, Grolier Division
Old Sherman Turnpike, Danbury, Connecticut 06816

Library of Congress Cataloging-in-Publication Data

Franck, Irene M.
     Tomatoes / Irene Franck and David Brownstone.
        p. cm. -- (Riches of the earth ; v. 14)
     Summary: Provides information about tomatoes and their importance in everyday life.
     Includes bibliographical references and index.
     ISBN 0-7172-5730-4 (set : alk. paper) -- ISBN 0-7172-5726-6 (vol. 14 : alk paper)
        1. Tomatoes--Juvenile literature [1. Tomatoes.] I. Brownstone, David M. II. Title.

  SB349.F63 2003
  635'.642--dc21
                                                                                    2003044089

Printed in the United States of America

Designed by K & P Publishing Services

Contents

Some of our most favorite foods are made with tomatoes. This pizza, for example, started with a flavorful tomato-based sauce on top of the crust, to which cheese, mushrooms, peppers, and other goodies were added.

A Favorite Food

Think pizza. Think spaghetti. Think ketchup. Think salsa. Some of our most favorite foods involve the tomato. Indeed, the tomato seems to be almost everywhere in our modern world.

Surprisingly, the tomato is rather a latecomer among foods. Humans have grown many other foods for thousands of years. However, in most parts of the world they have grown and eaten tomatoes only for a few centuries.

No matter—the tomato is making up for lost time. The average American today eats more than 25 pounds of tomatoes each year! And that's not counting the tomatoes Americans eat in ketchup, pizza and spaghetti sauces, soups, and other prepared dishes containing tomatoes.

One reason tomatoes are popular is that they can be used in so many ways. They can be eaten raw, cooked, or dried, and whole, sliced, diced, or as a paste, soup, or juice. Whatever their form, tomatoes retain their color and flavor, adding to almost any dish or meal. Today many cultures from all around the world have special dishes featuring tomatoes.

Tomatoes are also attractive and colorful. Even before northern Europeans started eating the tasty fruits, they grew tomatoes as ornamental plants in gardens or window boxes, because they looked so bright and pretty. (They didn't eat the fruit because they thought it was poisonous; see p. 13.)

Even today, when we know how delicious tomatoes can be, they are often used as much for their looks as their taste, as when slices of tomato or small cherry tomatoes are placed on lunch or dinner plates. Tomatoes are a key part of many salads, offering both flavor and color. Sliced tomatoes are also a popular addition to many sandwiches, such as a hamburger on a bun or a classic bacon, lettuce, and tomato sandwich.

Long a popular Hispanic dish, tomato salsa has now become a worldwide favorite, often with corn chips as shown here.

What Is a Tomato?

Tomatoes begin with yellow flowers like these. If all goes well, each flower will result in a tomato, which grows from the ovary deep inside the flower.

Is a tomato a fruit or a vegetable? The answer is: It's both at once. To biologists a food that contains fleshy pulp and seeds—as a tomato does—is called a *fruit*. However, in the everyday world, a plant food that is normally part of a main meal (rather than dessert) is generally called a *vegetable*. Some people call the tomato a *fruit vegetable*.

How a Tomato Grows

Each tomato plant grows from a single seed planted in soil. As the plant grows, buds develop at the ends of the branches. Each bud blossoms into a small yellow flower. The tomato fruit develops from a round section called the *ovary*, deep inside the flower.

The ovary contains small structures called *ovules*. In the fully grown tomato fruit these ovules will grow into seeds. For this to happen, the ovary must be *pollinated*—that is, it must receive some of a dustlike material called *pollen* that develops at the top of the flower. In fields or

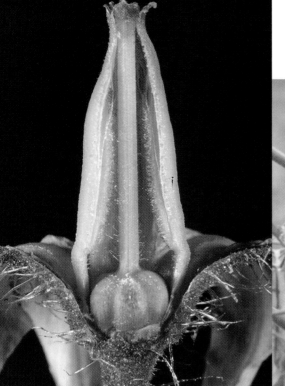

The tomato fruit grows from a round section called the ovary deep inside the yellow tomato flower, as shown at the bottom of this cross-section. For the tomato to grow, a dustlike substance called pollen must travel from the top of the flower down to the ovary.

The green leaves and stems of the tomato plant are covered with hair and have a distinctive odor, which many people find unpleasant. They are also poisonous, though the fruit is not.

gardens the pollen is often shaken down into the flower by the wind or the motion of insects. In a modern greenhouse or other shelter, gardeners sometimes vibrate, tap, or blow air on the plants to do the same thing.

In modern varieties of tomatoes grown in fields and gardens, the pollen usually comes from the plants' own flowers. They are called *self-pollinating*. However, in wild varieties the pollen may come from other tomato plants, perhaps carried by the wind or insects. These are said to be *cross-pollinated*.

Once the plant is pollinated, the tomato fruit begins to grow from the ovary, as other parts of the flower drop away. At first, the fruit

A tomato's seeds are found surrounded by a jellylike material in "pockets" (*locules*) between more solid parts of the tomato, as shown in these tomato cross-sections. From each of these seeds a new tomato can grow.

is small, hard, and green. Later it grows larger, softer, and tastier, and changes color, in most varieties to red.

The tomato plant's leaves and stems are covered with hairs and have a strong odor. They are also somewhat poisonous to eat, though the fruits are not. Some tomato plants grow like vines, while others grow more like shrubs (see p. 21).

As it grows, the tomato plant uses water and nutrients (nourishing substances) drawn in through its roots in the ground. Its green leaves also use sunlight, carbon dioxide (a common gas) from the air, and water to make various sugars, in the process called *photosynthesis*. The sweet-tasting sugars are *carbohydrates*, energy-supplying substances made of carbon, hydrogen, and oxygen. These sugars, primarily *glucose* and *fructose*, are the plant's main energy source.

Inside the skin the tomato's main bulk is made up of a fleshy pulp. It also includes many seeds. These are found in "pockets" (*locules*) surrounded by a jellylike substance, which contains most of the tomato's vitamin C. In some tomato varieties

Early in their growth tomatoes are green, like the ones shown here. They only turn red (or yellow or orange) when fully ripe. Sometimes tomatoes are picked somewhat green and ripen on the way to market.

the pockets are all of a similar size and shape and are spaced evenly inside the tomato. In other varieties the pockets have no standard shape or size and are scattered inside the tomato in a less organized way.

The final size of the tomato fruit depends on the variety. It can be as small as a cherry tomato (under an inch wide) to as large as a beefsteak tomato (several inches wide).

The shape of the tomato also varies. Most modern varieties are round or nearly so. However, some are shaped more like plums (longer than they are wide) or pears (wider on one end than the other).

Once the tomato reaches the usual size for its variety, it is said to be mature. The tomato then stops growing and can be picked, even if it is still green.

Whether picked or still on the plant, the tomato fruit then goes into the final stage of its life: ripening. At this time many chemical changes take place in the tomato fruit. These cause the tomato to become sweeter, softer, and tastier. These changes are reflected by changes in the fruit's color from green to red or, in some varieties, orange or yellow.

Good for You

The tomato is not as nutritious as many other vegetables. That is partly because a raw tomato is more than 90 percent water. However, people eat so many tomatoes and tomato products that these are a main source of some important vitamins and minerals.

Tomatoes are a very good source of vitamins A and C and the mineral potassium. *Carotenes*—colored substances that give tomato fruits their red, orange, or yellow color—help the body make even more vitamin A. Tomatoes also include smaller amounts of vitamins E and B complex (thiamine and riboflavin) and various minerals.

Tomatoes contain little of the important body-building substance

Tomatoes come in many shapes and sizes. These bright red plum tomatoes (left)—so called because they are roughly the size and shape of some plums—are for sale at a farmer's market. Below are Yellow Pear tomatoes, so called because they are roughly the size and shape of pears.

When tomatoes get very ripe, they get extremely soft and squishy, like this one that has been thrown against a wall. In centuries past rioters sometimes threw rotten tomatoes during protests.

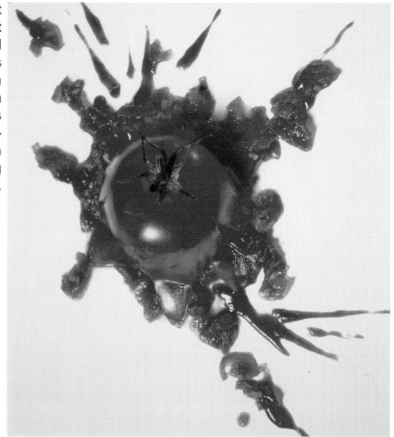

called *protein* (less than 1 percent, mostly in the seeds) and also little fat. They also contain only small amounts of *carbohydrates* (see p. 8), only about 3 to 5 percent. As a result, tomatoes are a good choice for people who are on a low-fat, low-carbohydrate diet.

The tomato's taste comes mainly from acids such as *malic acid* (found in many unripe fruits) and *citric acid* (the kind found in citrus fruits such as oranges or lemons), plus flavor-giving substances called *volatiles*.

These make the tomato's taste somewhat tart, especially when it is mixed with vinegar. To offset that, many cooks add sugar to tomato sauces. The use of sugar in tomato sauces is increasing. Some ketchups (see p. 28) are as much as 25 to 30 percent sugar!

The acids in tomatoes help keep harmful organisms from growing in the fruit or in foods made from it. This makes tomatoes good for various kinds of canning and preserves (see p. 28).

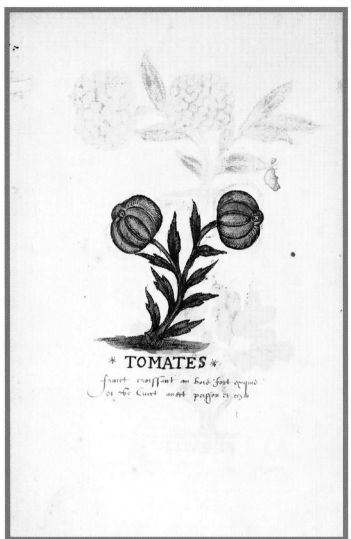

This drawing of tomatoes growing on a plant was made in the late 1500s, soon after the Spanish arrived in the Americas. It appeared in a French book, *Natural History of the Indies*. In English the caption reads: "Very exquisite fruit growing in the wood and being cooked with fish and meat."

What's in a Name?

Tomatoes and potatoes look and taste very different, but they are actually "cousins." Both originally came from South America (see p. 14). They are also part of the same plant family, which biologists call *Solanaceae*.

The Aztecs, who lived in what is now Mexico, gave the tomato plant the name *tomatl*. Shortly after the Spanish arrived in Mexico in the early 1500s, they brought the toma-to back to Europe. There it came to be called *tomate* (pronounced *toe-MAH-tuh*).

Over time—perhaps under the influence of the similar word *potato*—the spelling and pronunciation changed. Today we spell the name *tomato* and more often pronounce it *toe-MAY-toe*.

From Spain the tomato traveled elsewhere in Europe. The Italians adopted it enthusiastically. Indeed,

Tomatoes were long known as "love apples," from the French name *pomme d'amour*. **The name survived at least into the early 1900s, when Edna Boies Hopkins created this colored woodcut called** *Love Apples*.

when we think of Italian food today, we think first of tomatoes. The Italians called the tomato *pomo d'oro*, meaning *golden apple*. This may mean that the first tomatoes taken to Europe were yellow or orange. Some tomatoes are still those colors, though today most are red.

As the tomato traveled northward in Europe, the French gave it a new name: *pomme d'amour*. In English this was translated into *love apple*, and many early Americans used this name for the tomato.

Many northern Europeans, especially the British (and North American colonists), did not eat the tomato fruit because they thought it was poisonous. Why people believed this is unclear. The tomato does have some highly poisonous cousins in the *Solanaceae* family, such as belladonna (*deadly nightshade*). Also the tomato's green parts (stems and leaves) are mildly poisonous, though the fruit is not.

Though they did not eat tomatoes, northern Europeans grew tomato plants in their gardens and window boxes because they were pretty and colorful. Some also used the "love apple" as a medicine, as for healing cuts or sore eyes.

Modern biologists know the tomato under a different, scientific name: *Lycopersicon esculentum*. This roughly translates into "edible wolf's peach"!

The original wild tomatoes were about the size of modern cherry tomatoes, like these just picked from a community garden in Chicago.

Spreading and Improving Tomatoes

The tomato originally comes from the Andes Mountains of South America, in what is now Ecuador and northern Peru. Wild varieties of tomato still grow in that region. Native Americans apparently gathered and ate these small wild tomatoes.

Gradually the wild tomatoes spread more widely, including northward into Central America and Mexico. Native Americans in these regions were apparently the first to cultivate the tomato—that is, to deliberately grow it for food. These early farmers also began the long process of improving the tomato.

The wild tomatoes of South America were small yellow, orange, or red fruits, only about the size of modern cherries or cherry tomatoes. When Native-American farmers planted them for food, they chose seeds from the largest and best-tasting fruits to plant for the next year's crop (see p. 18). Over time this process developed larger, tastier tomatoes.

The same thing happened in Italy. The Spanish brought to Europe a tomato that was more ribbed and flat than round and smooth. It probably first arrived in Italy through the southern port of Naples, which in the 1500s was a Spanish territory.

In any case, the Italians adopted the tomato as their own. They are responsible for developing many different kinds of tomatoes of various colors, shapes, and sizes.

From Europe new and improved tomatoes spread around the world, including back to the Americas. New kinds of tomatoes and tomato dishes were introduced to southern North America by Spanish and

Pickles and Tomatoes, painted by Luis Eugenio Meléndez, shows what tomatoes looked like in Spain in the I700s. They were ribbed and flattish, rather than more smoothly round like modern tomatoes.

(Above) Genetic engineers are developing new varieties of tomatoes for specific purposes. These are Endless Summer tomatoes, designed for a better flavor and longer shelf life, though some people are concerned about possible long-term negative effects of genetic engineering. In the background is a printout of the tomato's genetic codes, which determine its growth and development. (Right) This tomato researcher is comparing Florida-grown Endless Summer tomatoes with others of the same variety grown in a greenhouse.

French colonists and immigrants. (The tomato had remained an important part of many kinds of dishes in Central and South America and in Mexico.)

The tomato spread much more slowly in the American colonies settled by people from the British Isles.

That is because well into the 1800s many of them still thought that the tomato was poisonous (see p. 13). Because of that, the tomato did not become widely popular in North America until late in the 1800s.

By the early 1900s, however, the tomato was on its way to becoming one of the most popular foods in North America. By the late 1900s it was one of the top half-dozen crops grown on commercial farms—and this did not count the tomatoes grown in millions of home gardens. In addition the tomato led the list of foods canned commercially, being processed into many different forms, including whole tomatoes, tomato juice, ketchup and other tomato-based sauces and pastes, and tomato soup (see p. 28).

Modern Changes

Modern scientists have made more improvements in the tomato. They have helped develop many of the large, fleshy, tasty tomato varieties grown today. One of the largest, the *beefsteak tomato*, can weigh as much as two pounds each!

Scientists have also developed new varieties of tomatoes for different purposes. Modern shoppers want tomatoes year-round, so scientists have developed tomatoes that grow in a wide range of climates and also in greenhouses (see p. 18). They have also developed tomatoes that can stand being harvested by machine or being picked by hand and then sent long distances to markets (see p. 24). Many tomatoes have also been developed primarily for looks.

Unfortunately, with the improvements also came losses. Some beautiful-looking tomatoes, able to travel long distances without obvious damage, have lost some of their famous taste.

Genetic Engineering

Many of today's new tomato varieties were developed using the age-old techniques of planting seeds from tomatoes with the most highly desirable qualities. Starting in the late 1900s, however, scientists began to make changes in the genes of the tomato. These genes form the basic set of biological codes that guide the growth and development of the tomato.

This kind of *genetic engineering* has developed new varieties of tomatoes with attractive characteristics. However, genetic engineering has also raised many concerns. Many people fear that tinkering with a plant's genetic codes might damage the environment, including the people who eat the tomatoes and products made from them. The long-term effects of such genetic changes are still unknown.

Growing Tomatoes

Modern tomato seedlings often start their lives growing in small containers inside greenhouses, which provide the plants with sunlight but allow temperature and humidity (amount of moisture) to be controlled.

In the tomato's original South American homeland, the climate was dry and the temperature was moderate, generally in the 60s and high 50s (in degrees Fahrenheit) during the growing season. Tomatoes are still sensitive to extremes of temperature and water. Tomato plants do not grow well where temperatures are too cold (under 50 degrees) or too hot (above 95 degrees), or if the soil has too much water. Under those conditions the plant may set (grow) fewer fruits. At the worst, frost or lack of moisture can kill the tomato plant.

Even so, modern improved tomatoes (see p. 17) can be successfully grown in a much wider range of climates then ever before. In the United States, for example, tomatoes are grown outdoors in every state except Alaska.

Extending the Growing Season

The tomato's growing season has been much extended by the use of *greenhouses* to grow seedlings (young plants grown from seeds). A greenhouse is a special structure, often built primarily of glass or plastic. This lets in the sunlight that

Greenhouses not only protect seedlings but are also used as a laboratory for scientists, who are trying to add some qualities from wild tomatoes to modern cultivated tomatoes.

plants need for growing (see p. 8) but allows the temperature and humidity (amount of moisture) to be controlled. This means that, even if it is cold outside, the greenhouse can keep the plants in their "comfort range."

Once the weather outside is warm enough, the tomato grower can take the seedlings out of the greenhouse and plant them in the ground outside, a process called *transplanting*. Some gardeners first plant the seedlings in an outdoor box called a *cold frame*. Though

unheated, it shields the seedlings somewhat from cold and wind. Other gardeners move the seedlings (often in trays of small containers) outside the greenhouse for a few hours a day before planting them in soil. These approaches give the seedlings a chance to adjust to outdoor conditions.

Even so, tomato growers must be very careful about temperature. Unexpectedly cold temperatures and late frost or snow can kill off the seedlings or cause tomato plants to set fewer fruits. To prevent this,

Sometimes other plants are planted as *mulch* between tomato plants. The hairy vetch planted as mulch here draws valuable nitrogen from the soil, lowers the soil temperature during the summer, and reduces weed growth and water loss.

tomato plants, providing such individual protection is generally too expensive. However, many farmers use *mulch*—protective matter such as straw or even plastic—on top of the soil between the plants. In addition to protecting the roots from too much cold, the mulch helps to keep down weeds (unwanted plants) and hold in moisture.

In some warm regions the tomato plant is a *perennial*—that is, it keeps on growing and developing flowers and fruits year after year. However, in most parts of the world the tomato is treated as an *annual*—that is, new plants are grown from seeds each year.

In warm regions growers can plant seeds directly into plowed ground, much as they would plant wheat or other seed crops. A machine called a *seed drill* can cut furrows (narrow trenches), measure and deposit seeds, and cover the furrows, all in a single pass.

However, most tomato growers today start with greenhouse seedlings. The growing season between

growers sometimes cover plants overnight, using "caps" of paper or plastic, water-filled fiberglass panels, cardboard boxes, plastic wrap around wire cages, or even hay or burlap.

Such protection requires a lot of work for a gardener. For commercial growers, with vast fields of transplanting and ripening varies widely, but is generally between 60 and 90 days.

How Tomatoes Grow

There are two types of tomato plants, based on how they grow. Some tomato plants grow without limit, until they are either uprooted or killed by frost. These are called *indeterminate* tomato plants. Kept inside a greenhouse under ideal conditions, these can grow to as much as 30 to 40 feet high in a year's time!

These vinelike tomato plants need to be supported, especially when they grow heavy with fruit. Gardeners and farmers often train them to grow on supports such as string, stakes, a circular metal cage, or an open wooden framework (*trellis*). These also keep the tomato fruits from coming into contact with the soil, which can damage them.

Indeterminate tomato plants are favored by home gardeners because the fruits do not ripen all at once. When tomatoes on the early branches are ripe, those on newer branches may still be green. This means that gardeners can have fresh tomatoes over many weeks. If grown commercially, tomatoes are picked by hand, since the pickers need to judge which tomatoes are ripe and which are not.

By contrast, the other type of tomato plant, called *determinate*, grows to a fixed size. When these

Vinelike *indeterminate* tomato plants must be supported, as here by stakes. They are picked by hand, rather than by machine, because pickers must judge which tomatoes are ripe enough to pick.

Tomatoes come in various shapes, sizes, and colors. Those that are grown in small gardens and vine-ripened are often not as completely smooth and red as commercially grown tomatoes, but they are often much tastier.

bushlike plants reach their usual size (depending on the variety), their stems and branches stop growing and the fruits develop. The tomato fruits all ripen at about the same time. Farmers who grow tomatoes for processing favor determinate plants because they can harvest all the tomatoes in a single pass, today generally by machine (see p. 24).

If determinate tomato plants are grown in a home garden, the gardener must either give away many tomatoes to others or plan to put some away as preserves (see p. 28). Otherwise, many will spoil because most will ripen at the same time.

Whatever the type of tomato, in garden or field, tomato growers often use mulch to protect plants (see p. 20). They also often use chemicals called *pesticides* to fight insects and diseases that can attack the tomato plant and damage or destroy its fruits. The problem is that pesticides can also damage the environment, so researchers are constantly seeking ways to grow tomatoes safely.

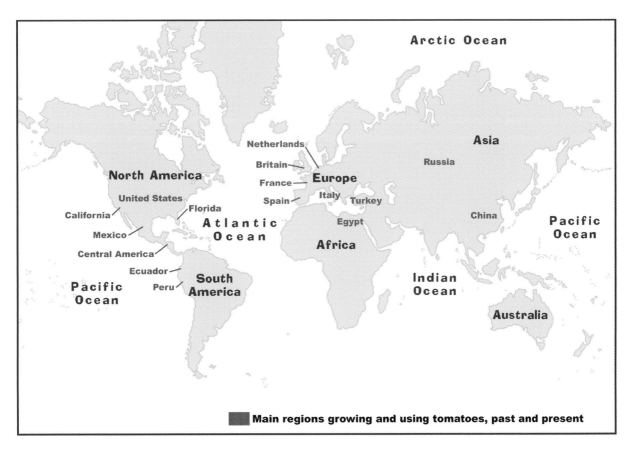

Arctic Ocean

Netherlands
Britain
France
Spain
Europe
Italy
Turkey
Asia
Russia

North America
United States
Florida
California
Mexico
Central America

Atlantic Ocean

Egypt
China

Pacific Ocean

Africa

Ecuador
Peru
South America

Pacific Ocean

Indian Ocean

Australia

■ **Main regions growing and using tomatoes, past and present**

Where Tomatoes Grow

Today tomatoes are grown all over the world. In many regions they are grown locally in gardens or small fields, for home use or for sale in local markets. However, most tomatoes today are grown on large commercial farms, often near major metropolitan areas.

The United States is the world's top tomato-producing country. Of the 50 states, California leads the way in growing tomatoes intended for processing (see p. 28), while Florida grows the most tomatoes to be sold fresh.

Other countries that grow large quantities of tomatoes include Russia, China, Italy, Mexico, Turkey, Egypt, and Spain. In northern Europe, especially in the Netherlands and Britain, tomatoes are widely grown in greenhouses. Surprisingly, tomatoes are not much grown in their original homeland, in the mountains of northern Peru and Ecuador.

Harvesting machines like this one (left) go through tomato fields at one pass, stripping them clean, like the field in the background. The harvested tomatoes are placed in a large bin and shipped to a nearby plant for processing into various kinds of tomato products.

Tomatoes intended for sale at markets are still usually picked by hand by farm workers as here (right) in Ontario, Canada. They are usually picked red-ripe only when they are going to be sold locally, because ripe tomatoes can be damaged during long travel.

Harvesting Tomatoes

For home gardeners harvesting tomatoes couldn't be easier. They just walk outside and pick a red, ripe tomato off the plant. One of a home gardener's great pleasures is eating such fresh homegrown tomatoes.

Tomatoes ripened on the vine are by far the tastiest of all tomatoes. That is why many people flock to farmer's markets for locally grown tomatoes in season.

However, many tomatoes sold for home use, as in large supermarkets, are not vine-ripened. Instead they are picked (often by hand) when they are full size but not completely ripe. Because the tomatoes are still rather hard, they can survive picking, packing, and shipping with little damage.

Various kinds of chemicals are later used to help the tomatoes ripen (see p. 9). One is a gas called *ethylene*, which is produced naturally by many fruits and vegetables. Another is a spray called *Ethephon* [(2-chloroethyl) phosphonic acid]. The tomatoes then ripen to their usual bright colors, but they lose some flavor and texture in the process.

Tomatoes for Processing

A large part of the commercial tomato crop is sent to processing factories, where they are made into tomato products of all sorts (see p. 28). When tomatoes are intended for processing, farmers usually grow determinate plants (see p. 21), because the tomatoes ripen at roughly the same time. These are harvested in a single pass by a machine that cuts off the whole plant at the soil level. The plants are then passed over a series of rods that shake the tomato fruits from their stems. The stems, plus loose soil and stones, fall back into the field.

Sometimes workers ride on the side of the harvesting machine. As tomatoes go by on a conveyor (continuously moving) belt, these workers sort the tomatoes, rejecting those that are unripe or too badly damaged, and also picking out the remaining stems and stones. Tomatoes are then sent quickly to nearby processing plants. Sometimes the sorting is done at the plant, instead of in the field.

Working on a cart at the back of a tomato-harvesting machine, these two women are sorting tomatoes, removing green or damaged ones. Sometimes this type of sorting is done at the processing plant.

25

Tasty Tomatoes

(Left) Tomatoes can be squeezed for a tasty juice. Often this is mixed with the juice of other vegetables, such as carrots and celery, for an even healthier and better-tasting drink. (Right) In many cultures around the world, raw tomatoes are marinated (soaked in vinegar or wine with spices). This is *bruschetta*, an Italian version of marinated diced tomatoes, served atop white bread.

Tomatoes can be eaten raw with nothing added or with just a little salt or lemon. Raw tomatoes can also be cut up and marinated—soaked in vinegar or wine with oil, spices, and herbs—to make special sauces. The resulting dishes include the Hispanic favorite *salsa*, which mixes tomatoes with onions and chili peppers, and the Italian dish *bruschetta*, which is marinated diced tomatoes served on crusty white bread.

Tomatoes may also be pickled—preserved and flavored in a bath of salty water or vinegar—to make a wide range of tasty relishes. Some people use ripe red tomatoes, but harder green tomatoes are also popular for relishes and preserves.

Uncooked tomatoes can also be cut into slices and dried in the open air, as is often done in Italy. The resulting sun-dried tomatoes are a popular snack on their own and a

Whether made at home from scratch or in a food-processing factory, spaghetti sauce starts with tomatoes. They are cooked down, as much of the liquid boils off, and flavored with onions, garlic, and other kinds of herbs and spices.

flavorful addition to many salads and other dishes.

Cooking Tomatoes

Tomatoes can also be cooked in many ways—baked, boiled, stewed, fried, and more. One of the oldest surviving descriptions of how tomatoes were eaten in earlier times comes from 1544; a traveler noted that Italians ate tomatoes fried in oil with salt and pepper. Fried tomatoes are still widely popular—including fried green tomatoes, not just red ripe ones.

Pieces of tomatoes are also added to many kinds of dishes around the world, from a Chinese stir fry to an Eastern European roast pork with tomatoes and sauerkraut. Tomatoes are an important part of many kinds of soups and stews, including the ever-popular tomato soup.

Tomatoes are also often cooked down, with many spices added, to make delicious sauces. The Italians, in particular, are famous for their flavorful tomato sauces to top many kinds of pasta and pizza dishes. Tomato sauces are a popular commercial product, including the enormously popular ketchup (see p. 28).

For many purposes, especially

Ketchup, Catsup, or Catchup

Can you imagine ketchup without tomatoes? The original ketchup was a salty, spicy fish sauce. The word is thought to come from a Malay or Thai word *kachiap*, perhaps originally from the Chinese *koe-chiap* or *ke-tsiap*, meaning brine (salty water) from pickled fish.

Ketchup has also been made with other main ingredients, including walnuts and cranberries. However, tomatoes made such a tasty sauce, they drove out all their competitors. Whether you spell the modern version *ketchup*, *catsup*, or even *catchup*, it is almost sure to feature tomatoes.

Modern scientists are developing tomatoes that contain more solids and less water. These are better for making ketchup, tomato soup, tomato paste, and all kinds of tomato-based sauces.

for sauces, tomatoes are first peeled and sometimes the seeds are also removed. At home this is done by hand using a knife, often after the tomato has been briefly dipped into very hot water to loosen the skin.

Processing Tomatoes

In factories tomatoes are generally peeled by machine, with the skins first being loosened by hot water or treated with various chemicals, which are then washed off.

Before peeling, tomatoes have been first carefully washed and sorted, again often by machine.

Tomato-processing factories are called *canneries* because most of the products are preserved in cans for later use. In the canning process foods are sealed in air-tight containers. These have been specially treated, often by boiling, to kill any harmful organisms that can cause the food to spoil and can sicken people who eat it.

Safe methods of canning were developed in the early 1800s, at first using jars. In rural areas some people still can tomatoes and other products in glass jars. However, most canning today is done in factories using tin cans (actually made of tin-coated steel).

Some tomatoes are canned whole, without further processing, so cooks can just open a can when fresh tomatoes are not available. Other tomatoes are processed in various ways, such as chopping or squeezing them into juice or paste (solids with much of the water taken out), all also by machine.

In some factories tomatoes are then moved on to be cooked into sauces, soups, stews, or other dishes. These are then packaged in various ways, sometimes frozen but most commonly canned, finally appearing in your local supermarket.

Canning tomatoes is big business. These tomatoes from California's fields have just arrived at a Sacramento cannery. They are being sorted and washed before being converted to everything from ketchup to soup to spaghetti sauce.

Words to Know

annual A type of plant that lives and grows for only one year, unlike a PERENNIAL.

belladonna: See DEADLY NIGHTSHADE.

cannery: See CANNING.

canning A method of processing foods and sealing them into specially treated, airtight containers such as cans, today often done in factories called *canneries*.

carbohydrates Chemical compounds (mixed substances) made of the elements (basic substances) carbon, hydrogen, and oxygen, in tomatoes mostly the sugars *glucose* and *fructose*.

carotenes Colored substances that give tomato fruits their red, orange, or yellow color.

citric acid A substance that helps give tomatoes their taste.

cold frame An unheated box placed over plants growing outside, to shield them somewhat from wind and extreme cold.

cross-pollinated: See POLLINATION.

deadly nightshade (belladonna) A highly poisonous member of the SOLANACEAE plant family.

determinate A type of tomato plant that grows only to a certain size (depending on the variety), unlike INDETERMINATE plants. The tomato fruits ripen at about the same time, making them attractive for commercial farming and machine harvesting.

fructose: See CARBOHYDRATES.

genetic engineering Making changes in tomato genes, the basic set of biological codes that guide the plant's growth and development, to create better qualities. The long-term effects of this are unknown.

glucose: See CARBOHYDRATES.

greenhouse A special structure, often of glass or plastic, for growing plants. It lets in the sunlight but allows temperature and moisture to be controlled.

indeterminate A type of tomato plant that grows like a vine without limit, until it is either uprooted or killed by frost. The tomato fruits ripen at different times, unlike those of DETERMINATE plants.

locules "Pockets" inside the fleshy pulp of tomatoes that contain the seeds and a jellylike substance.

love apple: See POMME D'AMOUR.

Lycopersicon esculentum The scientific name for the tomato. It roughly translates into "edible wolf's peach."

malic acid A substance that helps give tomatoes their taste.

mulch Protective matter such as straw, plastic, or other plants placed on or in the soil between the plants.

ovary A small round structure deep inside a tomato flower. It grows into the tomato fruit if it is pollinated (see POLLINATION).

ovules Small structures inside the OVARY of a tomato flower. If the ovary is pollinated (see POLLINATION), the ovules grow into tomato seeds, from which new tomato plants can grow.

perennial A kind of plant that remains alive and regrows year after year, unlike an ANNUAL.

pesticides Chemicals used to fight insects and diseases that can attack plants and damage or destroy their fruits.

photosynthesis The process by which plants use sunlight, carbon dioxide, and water to make CARBOHYDRATES.

pollination The process of transferring the dust-like material called *pollen* from the top of a flower to the OVARY in the bottom. Plants that receive pollen from their own flowers are called *self-pollinated*, like most modern tomatoes. However, many plants (including wild tomatoes) receive pollen from other plants; they are *cross-pollinated*.

pomme d'amour A French name for the tomato. In English this was translated as *love apple*.

pomo d'oro An Italian name for the tomato, meaning "golden apple."

ripening The final stage of a tomato's life, when it changes from a hard, green fruit to a softer, tastier reddish one.

seedling A young plant grown from seeds.

self-pollinated: See POLLINATION.

Solanaceae A family of plants that includes tomatoes, potatoes, and DEADLY NIGHTSHADE.

transplanting Moving a plant from one place to another, as from a GREENHOUSE to a garden.

volatile A substance that helps give tomatoes their taste.

On the Internet

The Internet has many interesting sites about tomatoes. The site addresses often change, so the best way to find current addresses is to go to a search site, such as www.yahoo.com. Type in a word or phrase, such as "tomato."

As this book was being written, websites about tomatoes included:

http://www.urbanext.uiuc.edu/veggies/tomato1.html
Watch Your Garden Grow - Tomato, from the University of Illinois Extension, offering information on growing tomatoes, including descriptions of many different sizes and varieties.

http://www.ars.usda.gov/is/tom/
Power Tomatoes, from the Agricultural Research Service of the U.S. Department of Agriculture, offering home gardeners or commercial growers information about how to grow more and better tomatoes, including links to the National Agricultural Library.

http://www.ianr.unl.edu/pubs/horticulture/g496.htm
Tomatoes in the Home Garden, from the Nebraska Cooperative Extension, offering information about when and how to plant and grow tomatoes.

http://www.tomato.org/
California Tomato Commission website, offering background information, news, tips, and recipes.

In Print

Your local library system will have various books on tomatoes. The following is just a sampling of them.

Gould, Wilbur A. *Tomato Production, Processing and Technology*, 3rd ed. Baltimore, MD: CTI Publications, 1992.
Hardgrave, Philip. *Growing Tomatoes*. New York: Avon, 1993.
The Harrowsmith Tomato Handbook. Jennifer Bennett, ed. Charlotte, VT: Camden House, 1986.
Jones, J. Benton, Jr. *Tomato Plant Culture: In the Field, Greenhouse, and Home Garden*. Boca Raton, FL: CRC Press, 1999.
Smith, Andrew F. *Souper Tomatoes: The Story of America's Favorite Food*. New Brunswick, NJ: Rutgers University Press, 2000.
_____. *The Tomato in America: Early History, Culture, and Cookery*. Urbana: University of Illinois Press, 2001.
Tarr, Yvonne Young. *The Tomato Book*. New York: Vintage, 1977.
The Tomato Crop: A Scientific Basis for Improvement. J. G. Atherton and J. Rudich, eds. London; New York: Chapman and Hall, 1986.
Van Nostrand's Scientific Encyclopedia, 8th ed., 2 vols. Douglas M. Considine and Glenn D. Considine, eds. New York: Van Nostrand Reinhold, 1995.
Vaughan, J. G., and C. A. Geissler. *The New Oxford Book of Plants*. New York: Oxford, 1997.

Index